"*You First* invites us to consider the mystical in our lives, the power of our own spiritual journey on this one Earth. Through poems and essays, Karen Luke Jackson imbues the ordinary cadence of this life—with its losses and loves and legacies—with the divine presence available to us all. This book showed me how to discover the sacred essence I yearn for but sometimes neglect to see."

—Mallory McDuff, author of *Our Last Best Act: Planning for the End of Our Lives to Protect the People and Places We Love*

"From her childhood baptism in Coochie Creek in South Georgia to her rebirth at a mikvah in Oregon years later, Jackson takes readers on a captivating, sensory-filled journey through country churches, sacred meadows, labyrinths, sequoia groves, and holy waters. As she navigates various life challenges–a divorce, the death of her parents, a major career shift, a health crisis–Jackson is awed by mystical experiences that help her make peace with the past and with the future. Seamlessly blending poetry and prose and propelled by a sense of deep searching, Jackson's work reads not like a sermon or academic treatise but like an invitation, a call to join her on a mesmerizing trek to the edge of this world and beyond."

—Jennifer McGaha, author of *The Joy Document: Creating a Midlife of Surprise and Delight*

"'That other life I might have fled my vows' writes Karen Jackson, but in this life, she spirals courageously towards the Mystery—opening, opening to what is luring her—the sacred in laurel thickets, women mystics, and bowls of soup. In writing both demanding and spacious, rooted in the body and dancing with the ineffable, Jackson cracks open doors to wonder and Love comes flooding in."

—Molly Bolton, author of *What Blooms in the Dark*

"While deeply personal, this collection of poems and essays by Karen Luke Jackson is resonant with universal themes. Reading it, I am suspended in wordless appreciation again and again. It is a volume to be savored in small portions. Prepare to be nourished,

and perhaps freed. Karen's reflections on her journey may loosen your ordinary constraints and permit you to embrace more fully your own life path."

—Marjorie J Thompson, author of *Soul Feast: An Invitation to the Christian Spiritual Life*

"*You First* is a treasure of poetry and prose that bears witness to love that accompanies us through loss, healing, and wonder. Karen Jackson writes with spiritual courage and contemplative depth, inviting readers to listen inwardly and embrace the deep connections that surpass our understanding."

—Kathryn McElveen, Executive Director, Center for Courage and Renewal

"'I am learning to trust / this path,' writes Karen Luke Jackson in 'Walking the Labyrinth,' a poem in her moving new book *You First*. A divorce in mid-life shakes up her life sufficiently to propel her into a life of pilgrimage to sacred spaces. The poems and prose in her marvelous new book tell the story of her mystical experiences along the way and offer us, her fortunate readers, an opportunity to reflect on our own spiritual journeys."

—Richard Chess, author of *The Loneliest Monk*

You First

You First

A Love That Will Not Let Me Go

KAREN LUKE JACKSON

RESOURCE *Publications* • Eugene, Oregon

YOU FIRST
A Love That Will Not Let Me Go

Resource Publications
An Imprint of Wipf and Stock Publishers
199 W. 8th Ave., Suite 3
Eugene, OR 97401

www.wipfandstock.com

PAPERBACK ISBN: 979-8-3852-6547-3
HARDCOVER ISBN: 979-8-3852-6548-0
EBOOK ISBN: 979-8-3852-6549-7

"How can I speak of my encounter with you in a way that others will believe me?

Let the words find you, you who have been hiding from them for so long."

—Richard Chess

Contents

Acknowledgments *xi*

Section One

Dear One of Many Names and No Name 3
As a Child 4
You First 5
Only Once Did I Ask You to Leave 7
The Word 8
Golden Arches 9
Essay: Adrift 10

Section Two

A Longing That Will Not Let Me Go 15
Who Believes a Woman's Tale 16
St. Columba's Isle 17
In a Parallel Life 18
Above the Atlantic 19
Essay: New Bearings: A Jubilee Pilgrimage to Iona 20

Section Three

Frozen Music 25
Noon Prayer in Salisbury Cathedral 26
Annunciation Retreat at St. James 28
As If I Could Keep You a Secret 29
Winter Lights 30

Reminder 31
Her Swaddled Promise 32
Essay: Sacred Meadows 33

Section Four

Repair My House 43
The Woman Whose Locks Francis Cut 44
Monastery of St. Clare 45
On Retreat, St. Francis Springs 46
Walking the Labyrinth 47
Essay: Chasing the Mystery, One Labyrinth at a Time 48

Section Five

After Compline 61
Ushered 62
if there are other lifetimes 63
A Litany for Ancestor Wisdom 64
Reading Rilke in Early Morning Light 66
I Want It Said of Me, As It Was of Him 67
Essay: Mikvah 68

Notes 75
Bibliography 85

Acknowledgments

I want to thank the editors of the journals that first published the following poems and essays, some of which have been revised for inclusion in this collection, as well as the Weymouth Center for the Arts and Humanities in Southern Pines, North Carolina, that provided a residency during which I compiled the poems and essays in this collection.

Alive Now—"As If I Could Keep You a Secret" (as "Handmaiden's Joy") and "Reminder"

Amethyst Review—"I Want It Said of Me, As It Was of Him" (as "In his last days, he leaked light")

Braided Way—"Sacred Meadows"

The Dewdrop—"Noon Prayer in Salisbury Cathedral"

Friends Journal—"A Litany for Ancestor Wisdom"

Hungryhearts—"New Bearings: A Jubilee Pilgrimage to Iona" (as "New Bearings")

The Rose in the World—"Walking the Labyrinth" (as "Jacob's Pillow")

Thin Places: An Anthology—"St. Columba's Isle"

Tiferet Journal—"Chasing the Mystery, One Labyrinth at a Time"

Tipton Poetry Journal—"Frozen Music"

Wild Roof Journal—"Ushered"

I also wish to express gratitude to Kathleen Calby, who first suggested I focus on poems about my spiritual experiences and helped me cross the finish line; to Eric Nelson, who offered invaluable guidance as I revised older poems and crafted new ones (he suggested adding the endnotes!); and to Barbara Sabol, who taught me nuances of the haibun form beyond what I could have imagined.

My writing journey has been enriched by memoirist Jennifer McGaha, whom I met in the Great Smokies Writing Program, and by other fellow writers and poets who critiqued these poems and essays in their various stages: Beth Beasley, Molly Bolton, Marion Starling Boyer, Kenneth Chamlee, Jane Curran, Anne Westbrook Green, Greg Lobas, Janisse Ray, Marjorie Thompson, and Emily Wilmer.

Beyond my writing circles, many brave souls have companioned me on this wild and wonderful spiritual journey:

—Courage & Renewal colleagues including John Fenner, coleader of contemplative retreats for more than twenty-five years, and his wife Claire, who supported our work; Parker J. Palmer, founder of the Center for Courage & Renewal, whose vision and books offered me a path forward when I left my job at the community college; Kathryn McElveen, whose current leadership of the Center models the core values the organization espouses; Elaine Sullivan, a beloved mentor who took me under her wings in Dallas, Texas, when I was first becoming a facilitator, and who swears we were nuns together in another lifetime; Karen Harding, whom I recognized as a kindred spirit when we met in Taos and she led the Dances of Universal Peace; and other fellow Circle of Trust® facilitators, Allison DeHart, Diane Petteway, Chris Johnson, Gayle Williams, Larry Petrovick, Anne and Tom Butler, Joseph Gaston, Sally Hare, Kathy Gille, Karen Noordhoff, and John Baird.

—Women companions, including Jaan Ferree, who coled a women's group and taught me about labyrinths; Charlotte Cleghorn, with whom North Carolina Arboretum outings continue to renew my spirit; Maureen Linneman, who cared for me during my divorce and introduced me to Sufi teacher Atum O'Kane; Jessie Wilder, who invited me to Lemon Bay Park and shared the work of eco-theologian Thomas Berry; Beth Maczka, who returned to divinity school to pursue research about Mary Magdalene; Tasha Vanderwerf, Arlene Russell, Carole Ball, Vicki Caldwell, and the other women at Trinity Presbyterian Church (Hendersonville, North Carolina), who comprised the first women's spiritual formation group I led, and who insisted on continuing the group when I left to teach at Appalachian State; Betty Blackerby, with whom deep conversations keep me digging; Marjorie Thompson, a dear friend and spiritual director who encouraged me to journal about my mystical experiences; and the sisters at the Monastery of St. Clare, especially Sister Mary, who hosted me at their retreat house for the first time on a New Year's Eve, even though their policy was not to welcome guests during the holidays. Sister Mary told me she could tell from my voice that I needed a place to be and could not turn me away!

—Lifelong friends, including David and Elissa Kaplan, who have walked beside me since college and shared much about their Jewish tradition (they inspired the mikvah experience) and Tonya Staufer and Ann Arida Talley, who have supported me through many life changes and are like sisters to me.

—House church members who, although we no longer meet, treasure the deep bonds that were nurtured in that environment. They include storyteller Diane Rhoades, dream worker Diana McKendree, artist Connie Knight, silence holder Richard Johnson, plant whisperer Lunita D'Arcy, and avid seeker Bob Walker. More recently, Sunday night prayer lodge members John and Carolyn Myers, Jim and Judith Nourse, Valerie Hack, and Barbara Hess Kovaz, who provided spiritual nurturance during the pandemic and my open-heart surgery, as did a new neighbor, Bhakhang Tulku Rinpoche, whose prayers blanket the Highland Lake community where I now live.

—People instrumental in helping me heal the body-soul connection include Bill Matthews, who first named my experiences as mystical; John White, who introduced me to meditation; Peake Dana, who dispatched me to the Abbey of Gethsemane; Dave Keenan, who shared the teachings of Ramakrishna; Denise Medved, whose NIA classes attest that dance is medicine; caregiver and prayer partner extraordinaire Rosie Hall; fellow tree-lover Roger Bass; supportive neighbors Meg and Michael Reim and Phillip and Karen Joy Moore; and medicine-wheel teacher Skye Anne Luke Taylor, who reaches across the pond from Ireland to walk with me.

—Younger people whose unique journeys I've been blessed to witness and whose gifts the world needs include Julie Merritt Lee, Josh Bledsoe, Aimée Bostwick, Chantal McKinney, Todd Weatherly, Terry Davis, David Weintraub, Linda Saturno, Audrey Kincaid Brendel, and Scottish sacred musician and interspiritual minister Simon de Voil, whose Birdsong Vespers provide nectar for the soul.

I also want to acknowledge the inspirited matter of soil, mushrooms, shrubs and trees, burrows, dens and nests, oceans, rivers and creeks, winds and stones that carry memories. Many places that cradled me on my spiritual journey are mentioned in this book. Three are not and I name them now: Kanuga Conference Center, where I have engaged in ongoing spiritual wrestling and received untold blessings; Big Glassy Mountain at the Carl Sandburg National Historic Site, where I continue to hike, sit in silence, and listen for the still, small voice; and the Park at Flat Rock, where turtles invite me to slow down and give thanks.

I ask forgiveness of my children, Kerri Ruth and Jonathan. Growing up, you had to contend with a mother who was not fully present to your needs.

To ancestors and beloved teachers who no longer inhabit this earth in human form, I honor you by adding your names: James and Ella Royal, Ruth Royal Peterson, Eloise and O. L. Luke, Elliott and Gwynedd Tucker, James Royal, Janis Luke Roberts, Ella Jim Martin, Don Kelley, Fay Coker Walker, Bennett and Mary Page Sims, Dave Knotts, Fran McKendree, Chip Berning, Victor D'Arcy, Lee Waters, and Linda Fowler.

Truly I have been,
am now, and trust I will always be
surrounded by a great cloud of witnesses.

Section One

Dear One of Many Names and No Name

Present, even when I am not,
you are a heart that needs no bypasses,
lungs that buoy oceans and scatter sand
into deserts. I do not know you

yet we have made love.
I cannot see you, yet your light pierces
my flesh, assures me you are near
even when I'm not sure I want you.

I long for a sign and fear I will get one,
that you will ask me, like the rich young ruler,
to abandon the privilege I cling to. And so,
at times I crouch in closets, behind stairs.

But there is no escape. Even as I flee,
you are at my side shielding me.

As a Child

I snuck into the white country church while other children played chase outside. Sitting in the back pew, waving a funeral fan to cool my face, I watched men and women on opposite sides take annual communion: a bite of unleavened bread that my aunt who baked it pronounced tasteless as paper; a thimble sip of wine, my uncle's homemade blackberry. I hungered for your body, your blood, so mesmerized was I by the story Elder Thomas had spun from the pulpit earlier that morning, his tan coat unbuttoned, a lock of auburn hair banging his brow. A story about the last supper which sealed your fate and twenty centuries later molded mine. We were Baptist. Not Southern, Free Will, or Missionary. Not even Old Liner. Heavens no. We were Progressive Primitive Baptist, an oxymoron I later learned. We let women teach Sunday School. Washed feet. Fasted for rain.

You loved me first, the burning in my heart proof enough I was one of the elect. No hellfire to fear when I sang of an old rugged cross. You knew my sins before I confessed: the hateful words I hurled at my mother, not cleaning my plate while children in China starved. And my burdens: looking after my younger sister when I wanted to ride my bike. Your blood washed me clean; no priest needed. You said *let the children come*. The next week, dressed in white, I waded into Coochie Creek.

dawn chorus
a fledgling
joins the flock

You First

appeared after surgery, descended
through the crown of my head, settled
like a blanket over my chest.
I'd just learned my husband
had a lover. After warming my torso,
you left through the soles of my feet.
I knew, in time, I'd recover.

Scaling the face of Grandfather Mountain
years later, newfound suitor by my side,
a familiar tingle crept my shoulder blades,
announced your presence. *Attention*,
I'd come to call you. I feigned fatigue,
perched on a boulder and waited
for him to forge ahead before
welcoming the slow flush of fire.

I dared not share that you and I
had floated in meadows weighted
with the scent of lavender; spiraled
through galaxies in a black limousine.
Nor could I speak of how
we once circled the universe
watching souls spark from dying stars.

Then one day on a church playground,
you led me from Texas seesaws
and merry-go-rounds down
into my grandmother's crypt.
There we made love.
Afterward, you baptized me
in a pool of blood.

I would have gone mad
had I not heard of
Julian. Teresa. Hildegard.

Only Once Did I Ask You to Leave

and you did.

I believed
my body, my family,
my work
could not weather
your blaze.

In your absence
I shivered
as frigid as the outer space
where you orbited
waiting

until I begged
for your return.

The Word

My spine hackled like a dog's
when a friend called me a mystic. The label
conjured medieval battles, burnings at stakes,
heresies, witches.

But what else
could explain a grizzly old god
steering a buckboard, me bouncing
in the back,

or my watching a patient's soul
rise from her body in a hospital bed,
being caught up in the third heaven
as Paul writes.

Not me, I joked,
all the while fearing
someone might find
my journals.
Read them.

Golden Arches

I nose the car into the parking lot and enter a world of burgers and fries. I'm grateful for a place to rest and hungry for company, even that of strangers. As a young woman, I often went alone to movie theaters or churches when I needed to be in the presence of others. Now I frequent fast food places. On my way to be interviewed for a temporary teaching position, I'm once again traveling solo. I glance around. The sun has just crested the Blue Ridge Mountains. A few early comers standing in line in front of me exchange hellos. I step toward the counter, order coffee and a sausage biscuit.

Before walking my tray to a table, I ask for the real stuff rather than the powdered creamer provided. A teenager with sleep in his eyes hands me an open carton of low-fat milk. *Use what you need* he says. *If only I knew what I needed* I think as I pour liquid into what looks like mud and hand the carton back. Seated, I offer a quick blessing. This brew and bread, even though the biscuit is served in a filet of fish wrapper, is sustenance for my journey. I eat in silence, rise to toss my trash into a waste bin, and pull the keys from my pocket. I'm expected on campus by noon. Outside, air stings my cheeks. I slide behind the wheel, click the seat belt, and edge the car into traffic between a silver sedan and a white SUV.

roadside skid marks
clumps of daisies
wild with questions

Adrift

"God does not demand that we . . . lose ourselves and turn from all that is not him. God needs nothing, asks nothing and demands nothing, like the stars. It is a life with God that demands these things."—*Annie Dillard*

When I was in my forties, things that moored me in this world began to slip away. My husband's affair frayed our marriage. Cancer claimed a close friend. My livelihood became shaky. Nothing unusual during a midlife storm.

What *was* unusual, however, were the unexplainable experiences I began having—feeling enveloped in a divine love, being transported to underground catacombs and sacred meadows, and worshiping at altars I didn't recognize. Such happenings occurred at home washing dishes, on walks in the woods, in lucid dreams. Then one day at work, while at the computer drafting a letter, I was ambushed. Scenes of a medieval battle flashed in my head. I saw myself (could I have actually been there?) seated behind a knight on a white stallion, my arms gripping his armor. While witnessing unbelievable carnage, I feared a colleague might knock on my door. I don't know how long I inhabited two worlds. I only know the scene faded.

Mental illness ran in my family. Bipolar disorder. Paranoia. Schizophrenia. The increasing frequency of these out-of-body trips made me wonder if I was losing my mind. I'd worked with a therapist for a year attempting to salvage the marriage. We'd built enough trust that during a session I found myself describing one of these episodes.

"You're not crazy," he reassured. "You're holding a full-time job, teaching Sunday School, and handling the family finances. People from many spiritual traditions have such experiences. They're called mystical."

I remember startling at the word "mystical," still afraid and wishing I could rewind our conversation. If no one else knew, maybe the strange occurrences would cease. But the genie was out of the bottle.

"I can recommend a book or two that might offer some insight," he said, reaching for a notepad. Then he added, "These visitations are gifts. Learning to live with them will be your biggest challenge."

About the same time, I ran across Annie Dillard's essay "An Expedition to the Pole." Reading it, I felt a kinship with those Arctic and Antarctic explorers who, when their vessels became trapped in pack ice, abandoned ship, lugging not heavy coats or extra blankets but books, keepsakes, and silver tableware. Irretrievably lost, these men set up tents on floes for shelter.

I too was lost, my life foundered in its own pack ice. Abandoning ship, I set up shelter for myself and my son in the only home he'd known. My new financial situation wouldn't allow us to stay there long, but I wanted to provide a stable environment until he graduated from high school. As hope of salvaging my old life faded, I still did the grocery shopping, washed clothes, and went to work each day.

While the men waited to be rescued, did they long to be back in the world from which they'd sailed? I did. I ached to return to the days when my people were preachers, farmers, and mouth-watering cooks, to the summers I picked beans with my aunts and ran barefoot through cornfields and creeks. Like those explorers, however, I found myself on a floe with no landmarks or compass to guide me, no horizon to help me gain my bearing, drifting further from what I once knew. The ice-laden world, the freezing cold, took no notice of me.

Eventually I had to choose, as did those men. Remain bundled in the tent slowly dying or rip open my clothes and venture outside? They knew leaving would bring a quicker end to their suffering. I too desired a quicker end, but I fantasized that my leaving would be different: that if I wandered long and far enough, my frozen wasteland would become a tropical rainforest. Gentle breezes would replace frigid blasts. I would wake one morning free of worries and doubts.

Love without objects, Dillard extols, yet objects abound. And with objects come attachments, like the one I have to the recurring sensation that prickles the left shoulder blade above my heart. "Attention" is the name I gave that phenomenon which seems to be messaging me: *You are not alone.* I've become attached to these visits, yet I never know when they will come. When that lifeline is absent for long periods of time, I feel stranded like those men near the North Pole, disoriented souls drifting closer to nothingness.

And so, before I go, confessions are in order. Perhaps there is a perfect world where love without objects exists, but I am human. I still desire to have and to hold, to be had and held. I tuck my photos, my journals, the family silver under my arms and stumble from the tent like those lost sailors wandering in a sea of colorless stripes. Here, where ice blinds the horizon, I can no longer distinguish sky from land, heaven from earth.

Section Two

A Longing That Will Not Let Me Go

A lifetime, I've wandered forests,
wound labyrinths, retreated
to monasteries seeking
lyrics like the psalmist,
a song like Mother Mary's,
a way to witness
as did the Magdalen.

Who Believes a Woman's Tale

for Beth

Men scoffed at Mary and her towering news
but her face shone so bright, how could they doubt
He is risen!   *An idle tale.*   *Certain to be fallout.*

Apostles in hiding refused Mary's good news
about an empty tomb   *Body must have been moved.*
save Peter who ran to see what she touted.

Some scoff that a woman first bore the good news,
her face bright with his light.   About that, no doubt.

St. Columba's Isle

The stone bench in the abbey courtyard
offers solace as I come
to say farewell. First light
creeps across water I will cross
today, my blouse damp with morning dew,
my heart freshened, brimming.

Centuries ago,
praying men drifted
in coracles to this shore.
Monks were martyred
before pilgrims
like me flocked
to the Celtic crosses,
splashed in a well
of eternal youth, or
searched for an earthen
circle, site
of a hermit's cell.

Heavy in my bag,
from Iona's southern tip,
the oldest rocks on earth.
When wet, they glisten
rainbows, like I glow now.

In a Parallel Life

If I'd been born Catholic in Italy or Ireland,
I might have betrothed myself to a lover
who wooed women to convents and
monasteries, rather than wed a lawyer

from North Carolina whose mother
courted me til I walked down the aisle. There,
I'd have prayed with Clare or Brigid,
stirred porridge and tinctured herbs

rather than driven school carpools
and delivered Meals on Wheels. And in
that other life I might have fled my vows,
as I did in this one, but I never

would've mothered a daughter who feeds
hungry children. A son who pictures
mountain ridges flushed in rhododendron.

Above the Atlantic

the plane jettisons fuel, circles back toward Gatwick. A voice reminds us how to brace for a crash, slide down chutes. Some peer out windows. Others finger rosaries. Seat belted among strangers, I replay my fiftieth birthday on Iona. Mourning a divorce, I chanted in the restored abbey, wept in the nunnery's ruins, and sheltered beside Celtic crosses. The last afternoon, wind whipping my jacket at St. Columba's Bay, I picked up a stone, infused it with useless regrets, and tossed it into the sea. Then I reached for a pebble streaked with mermaid tears, named blessings to usher me home, and dropped the talisman into my pocket. As the approach begins, I take solace; my affairs are in order, my children grown, unlike the child in the next aisle clutching his mother's neck. I secure the table tray, retrieve the pebble, and grip it in my palm.

red ants swarm
from their mound
first responders

Landing gears thump. Fire trucks roll away. In the airport lounge, waiting for repairs to the plane, I down a whiskey.

New Bearings: A Jubilee Pilgrimage to Iona

"To journey and to be transformed
by the journey
is to be a pilgrim."—*Mark Nepo*

From the moment I learned of Iona's existence off the coast of Scotland, I had an inexplicable longing to visit. So, in 2000, when an Episcopal conference center in my hometown announced a pilgrimage from Canterbury to Iona, I leapt at the prospect of traveling to that sacred island, not as tourist, but as pilgrim.

The timing seemed providential. In 1999, a Poor Clare Sister who knew the radical shifts occurring in my life recommended I observe my upcoming year of jubilee. I had tried to rest in God's care as I finalized a divorce, resigned from work at a community college, and put the family home up for sale. Going on pilgrimage, however, seemed to be the celebration I needed to bring my observance to a close.

The house sold four weeks before we were to depart. I put what remained of my life's accoutrements in storage and moved into a 400-square-foot garage apartment until I could regain my bearings. When I boarded the plane for London, I thought about Columba, who established the first Christian community on Iona. In 563 CE, he and his monks departed Ireland in coracles, circular dish-like boats without anchors or oars, praying God's wind would carry them to a new life. Now I was uttering the same prayer.

Our trip was fourteen days long, seven days visiting cathedrals in England and Scotland, five days on the island of Iona, then two for the trip back home. We began at Canterbury Cathedral, the center of the Anglican world, then visited Salisbury, Coventry, and Carlisle Cathedrals before crossing the threshold of water and islands from Oban to Iona. The farther behind I left the pomp and institutional trappings of Canterbury and the closer I came to the simplicity of the small island community, the more comfortable I felt.

The day the ferry transported our group from the Isle of Mull to Iona, the sea was so choppy that the boat could not dock. I disembarked in several feet of water, climbed onto dry land, and dragged my luggage up a paved path to the St. Columba Hotel. There I was given a single room the size of a prayer closet.

Time spent in this "thin place" was full of God's constantly changing glory. Showers surprised us with double rainbows, then both rain and rainbows vanished. Footpaths beckoned us to explore the small island's farms, marshes, and ruins. Pebbled beaches provided a playground of colored stones to delight our senses.

I engaged in typical activities for an Iona pilgrim—resting, praying, reading Scripture, and even ringing the abbey bells that call people to worship. But one particular experience proved to be a pivotal moment of transformation during my time on the island.

The afternoon of the day before we were to leave, a younger woman and I got lost hiking. In our three hours of trudging through bogs, climbing over rocks, and crawling under fences, we stumbled upon the hermit's cell. Several of us had looked for this landmark earlier in the week but had been unable to locate the site where monks retreated from community life to spend time alone with God.

The minute I spotted the small circular ruin, I knew what it was. Mounds of earth formed a rough chair and a bed where a smooth stone served as a pillow. We entered that ring without a word. I sat in the chair and she lay on the bed. Sheltered from the sea by two rises, we heard nothing except an occasional bird flapping overhead or insect buzzing nearby. So isolated, so alive in that place, I felt cloaked by a holy warmth.

Early the next morning, I stole away into the abbey courtyard to say my goodbyes to this sacred island. I sat there humming "This is the Body of Christ" while pigeons cooed in the rafters. This was the day I was to begin my journey back to family, friends, and an unknown future. I was at peace and all was well.

Section Two

Back home I found myself on another pilgrimage, one that embraced the wonders of my own region, the mountains of Western North Carolina. Leaving and returning had sharpened my senses. I began walking the ridges and valleys, more open to holy moments. And they came. In a laurel thicket flush with pink. Near a patch of bloodroot when a cardinal rendered a morning song. Beside the sparkle and gush of Moore Cove Waterfall.

Section Three

Frozen Music

Baffled in high school
geometry by isosceles
triangles, algebraic formulas
and a theorem Pythagoras
handed down, I had no clue
mathematics and music
share a pattern
of perfect intervals,
ratios used to design
vaults and chancels
in Gothic cathedrals and
Cistercian abbeys, lilting
columns of draped stone,
frozen music. Too young then,
I was unattuned to the clefs,
anatomy and overtones
that loosen ligaments,
wobble bones, evoke pain
or bliss, depending upon
how jarring or sublime
the fatal kiss.

Noon Prayer in Salisbury Cathedral

murmurs   flood silence
      rebound
            from chill marked stone

the Our Father
      uttered   whispered   sung
            in hundreds   of tongues

by guests   guards   guides
                              statue still

whose chants
      swirl nave   chancel
                  lancet windows
      transform   gray walls
                  into gold transcendence

while angles and angels
            funnel praise and petitions
      up the tower's spiral stairs

            past peregrines and swifts
                  nesting in its spire, still scaffolded
                        from recent repairs

                        prayers that bathe the close
                  blanket Salisbury's Plain
      where sarsens and bluestones
                  echo   reply

for in the beginning   sound
gave rise
to brine and sap
and bone

a hum   a buzz   a swell
of birth cries

Annunciation Retreat at St. James

for Charlotte

Parishioners drift on a sea of silence,
their shoulders slumped, their faces
freighted with frowns.

Morning meditations: icons and paintings.
Gabriel's wings shadow Mary.
Dali renders the teen awe-struck.

In the quiet: followers of the long-awaited
and ever-present Christ Child
release their stories of *not enough*.

At lunch: Worshipers slurp butternut
squash soup as sun streams stained glass
windows in the fellowship hall.

An orange glow feeds
bodies of growing light.

As If I Could Keep You a Secret

Like the whoosh of grain spilling
        from a silo filled to overflowing
your blessings rain over me

        flush my body with a heat that blushes
        through the folds of my flesh.

Such extravagance robs me of breath
        frees me   of guilt   of fear   of any need
to explain. Shameless with adoration

        I yield, flailing
        in your love.

Winter Lights

after Mark Burrows, "Nine Forms of Light"

Fires blazing on mountain trails,
   among sand dunes, in alley trash cans.

Blue tubes
   ghosting ERs.

High beams blinding drivers
   headed home to star-strung wreaths.

Headlamps on miners' helmets
   shafting wormholes.

In a chilled shack, a bare bulb
   flickering above a naked table.

Streetlights yellowing a rusted van,
   its family inside shivering.

On purple linen, a white candle
   not yet lit.

Reminder

Fatigue, illness,
shortened days,
waves of loneliness.
Deep ache
for human form
to fill void.

Such longing
Advent's gift—
a battering
of the heart
meant to turn
us around,
bring us back
to you.

Her Swaddled Promise

In homes and churches, on mantles and communion tables,
nestled between blue-green needles and poisonous red berries,

Mary waits for her babe as she once did in a cave or stable
when there were no churches or communion tables.

The birth of that child, her swaddled promise, not a fable
like Santa who hoists a red bag, but we, unable

to pause in our homes and churches, at communion tables
miss Mary nestled between needles and berries.

Sacred Meadows

"Often I am permitted to return to a meadow . . ."—*Robert Duncan*

"Consider yourself hugged," Linda whispered in a raspy voice as I entered the room. My friend lay propped on white pillows in a borrowed hospital bed, her brown page boy hair tucked behind her ears. Cancer had feasted on her bones until she could no longer raise her arms. Even in her weakened state, she wiggled her fingers in a wave.

"What can I do for you?" I asked, knowing little could be done, other than bringing meals for her husband and her two estranged daughters, women in their twenties, who had come to see their mother before she died.

"Just sit here a while, by my side, so I can hear you," she said.

I lowered myself into a straight-backed chair and lifted her hand into mine.

"Does it hurt for me to touch you?"

"Not if you're gentle," she replied, closing her eyes as if our brief exchange had sapped all the energy she had stored for such visits.

After a few minutes of labored breathing, Linda broke the silence. "I want to tell you some things I've never shared with anyone."

"You probably need to rest," I protested.

"No. I need to get them off my chest, and I don't want to burden my daughters. They've been through enough already."

For several years, Linda and I had worked together in my husband Frank's law office. Hiring her as a paralegal was one of his best decisions. A nurse by training, she could ferret out medical records for personal injury and worker's compensation cases that gave him an advantage negotiating with adjusters and presenting evidence to a jury. Linda was, as Frank often told her, "worth her weight in gold."

During the time we'd known each other, she and I had celebrated each anniversary the doctors pronounced her breast cancer still in remission. But I knew little about Linda's earlier life in Florida.

"Did I ever tell you my mother was mentally ill?" she began. "When I was a little girl, she came after me with a butcher knife. Paranoid schizophrenia. Didn't know who I was."

"A cousin of mine lived through the same thing with her mom," I said, hoping the words would reassure her.

Linda went on. "That's why the divorce was a nightmare. My husband was a physician. He knew my family history. When I told him I was leaving, he threatened to have me committed."

"Could he have done that?" I asked.

"The marriage was a mistake. I suffered from depression. He told me, with his connections, I didn't stand a chance. And if I spent time in a mental institution, no judge would ever let me have the girls."

Linda paused to rest. When she resumed, her words came more slowly, as if she were reliving the scene.

"'Walk away,' he said. 'Make it easy on yourself and everyone else.' So that's what I did." Her eyes, ringed with dark circles, implored me to understand.

"You made the best decision you could at the time, Linda."

"Maybe. The girls were so young. I couldn't fight him and win . . . and I knew he'd be able to provide for them better than I ever could."

She exhaled, coughed. I could hear the rattle in her chest.

"Even if I'd lost, Karen, I wish I'd tried. I've never forgiven myself for signing over custody. And they haven't either."

As I lightly stroked her fingers, her body mustered a few meager tears. Once again, her eyelids closed, her head sank deeper into the pillow, and she drifted into what I presumed was sleep.

How long I remained in that chair, holding her hand, I don't know. Five minutes or fifty, it doesn't matter. Nor do I know whether my eyes were open or closed during that time. What matters is what happened. The walls of the room seemed to expand, become fluid, and dissolve. The air pulsed around me. Time slowed, then I was no longer "in time."

At some point, my surroundings came into focus again, and I glanced at Linda. She still seemed to be resting, so I picked up my purse and began to tiptoe out of the room.

"Wait, Karen."

I turned to see her eyes open wide. Her face hinted of a smile.

"Were you there?" she asked.

"Where?"

"The meadow. I was a child again, running and skipping in a field of tall grass. You were there with me. Did you see the wildflowers?" Her eyes flared with joy. "And that breeze, that wonderful breeze blowing through our hair!"

"I wasn't in the meadow, Linda, but I sensed something precious was happening. I can imagine you romping and playing there."

I don't remember the drive home. When I pulled into the garage and climbed out of the station wagon, I felt weightless, as if my feet no longer touched the ground.

Opening the back door, I found Frank sitting at the kitchen table. His glasses rested beside a file on which he'd been working. "You were gone a lot longer than I expected," he said. "I was afraid something bad had happened. How's Linda?"

Right then, I wish I'd asked him if he noticed anything different about me, if light were shining through my pores. Instead, we sat sipping sweet tea on our screened-in porch while I recounted details of the afternoon visit. After listening, Frank went upstairs and returned with a paperback novel entitled *Shibumi*. Locating a dog-eared page, he read aloud a passage that described a floating meadow experience.

"Was it like this?"

"I don't know. I wasn't in the meadow, Frank. All I can tell you is something happened to me while Linda was there."

That explanation was the only one I could provide. At the time, I didn't know the words "numinous" or "unitive." I'd grown up hearing older family members and lay ministers talk about how Spirit moves, touches our lives, comforts and guides us. Sometimes they'd refer to that presence as God, at other times the Holy Ghost. What had happened during my visit with Linda was outside rational understanding, but of two things I was sure: I was far too peaceful to be crazy, and nothing obvious in the external world had changed.

Linda died a few days later. By the time I attended her funeral, my weightless state had dissipated, but her parting gift lingered: an introduction to another realm where every cell in my bones and blood had been recalibrated. I knew my path forward had to embrace this new embodiment of divine mystery and love. I just couldn't fathom how.

A year later, the meadow reappeared during a Sunday morning worship service in a small Presbyterian church. I was emptying my mind of its usual "to-do" list during the silent meditation preceding the sermon when an image flashed into my consciousness. A young girl was running through a beautiful field, her hair flowing in the wind, the same scene Linda had described before her death. I sensed my friend's presence nearby. In the next image, two girls skipped hand in hand up a rise. In some inexplicable way, Linda had come to visit, and a part of me was in that landscape with her.

When the organ sounded the first notes of the doxology, the music startled me back into the sanctuary. I had missed the entire sermon. Again, the gift of the meadow left me floating and speechless. To avoid conversation, I slipped out of the church during the closing hymn. When I got home, I didn't mention the episode to my husband and, after a quick lunch, took a long walk in the neighborhood, absorbing light that streamed through the hemlock trees and rhododendron thickets.

In my childhood I hungered for sacred spaces—an empty church, stand of pines, or my backyard where stars glittered like diamonds in the indigo night sky. Pajama-clad, I would lie on the grass, stare at the constellations, and converse with whoever was "up there," unaware of time passing.

Such communion experiences lessened and eventually disappeared as I progressed through school, married, worked, and raised children. Somehow my friend's death and subsequent visit reopened a portal to that holy dimension. But her gift also left me with a dilemma.

As a Christian, I'd participated in the usual religious activities—attended church, prayed, taught Sunday School, and tried to comprehend Scripture and doctrinal points. The sacred occurrences with Linda fell outside that framework. They were too fragile, transcendent, and intimate to share; and honestly, I feared being considered suspect if I spoke about them. So, I held them close to my heart, wondering and wrestling with the fact that they were an undeniable part of my life.

Two years after Linda's death, surgery to repair a ruptured disc confined me for several weeks in my upstairs bedroom. Depressed that my marriage was floundering, I feared the future and had stopped eating. Early one morning, lying in bed, I was levitated into the back of a buckboard and transported to Linda's meadow. Once there, a gentle warmth entered the crown of my head, spread throughout my body, and exited through the bottom of my feet. Then, like a rising tide, a loving presence filled me and the whole room with healing light. That visit gave me enough energy to say yes to life, recover from the surgery, and weather the subsequent family upheaval.

The following summer, I saw a painting at a sidewalk art sale of what had now become *my* sacred meadow. I asked the artist to tell me about the scene.

"I was taken there several times while being treated for cancer," she said. "It was my sanctuary."

"I've been in that meadow too," I told her.

Each time I find myself transported to the meadow, familiar landmarks welcome me. At the highest point, a large, smooth, granite rock rises gently from the earth, providing a place for me to rest and soak in warm, radiant light. A short hike from the rock leads to a clear pond from which other animals and I drink. Streams feeding this watering spot meander through fields of lime-green, knee-high grass.

Sometimes daisies bloom or parts of the meadow blaze with wildflowers, as Linda first described. At other times, a golden haze bathes everything. Friends and loved ones, living and dead, join me occasionally, but most of the time I'm alone. I cannot see beyond the edges of the meadow but have been told by others who've visited that holy place that forests, caves, and underground rivers exist nearby.

Although I long to be in the meadow more often, I cannot go there of my own accord. These mystical moments seldom occur in the context of a guided meditation or in response to prayer. When the doorway opens and I am permitted to return to this place I can only call "beyond," I breathe in love, timelessness, and awe. In an otherworldly silence, divine breezes brush my skin. I know I am home.

At first I considered my meadow experiences rare. Over time, however, synchronistic conversations with others and reading published accounts have convinced me they are not limited to a chosen few.

For example, Jim Robbins' book *The Man Who Planted Trees* includes Plato's report of the near-death experience of a soldier named Er. After dying in battle, Er ascended to "a celestial realm where he saw a brilliant rainbow shaft in the meadows of heaven and watched as other souls chose a new life in which to be reborn." Ten days later, when dead bodies were being collected, Er regained consciousness and told his story.

A meadow also figures prominently in a 1995 account by contemplative theologian and psychologist Gerald May. In journal notes recorded while hospitalized during chemotherapy, May relates his vision. "God has placed me upon a promontory and has spread out before me a small version of the universe. It is a beautiful rolling meadow, and I am meant to see every part of it . . . the angels are everywhere; there is nowhere outside God's protection."

Closer to home, a friend in my women's circle shared that in a morning meditation, she'd pictured piling all her worries into a wheelbarrow and pushing them up a hill to the cross on which Jesus hung. As she left the wheelbarrow of burdens at the foot of the cross, she was free to walk in a holy field surrounded by friends and beautiful light.

Eager to know more, I asked, "Have you been in that place before?"

"Yes," she responded. "Last year." That's all she would say.

My friend's journey may have been too fresh and sacred to air more of it out loud, but my trips had been recurring for years. We were both members of a church which honed theological arguments, took vigorous stands on social justice issues, and professed a belief in the mystical body of Christ. We'd taught each other's children in Sunday School classes and broken bread together. So why did I hold back?

Several weeks after her call, I found another meadow account in a book I'd checked out of our church's library, *Thinking with Your Soul: Spiritual Intelligence and Why It Matters*. Author Richard N. Wolman had invited participants in a pilot study at Harvard University to describe a personal transformative spiritual experience. One mother whose eleven-year-old son was diagnosed with an inoperable malignant tumor shared a dream which she likened to a near-death experience:

> I was in a beautiful meadow, walking toward a small stream only two or three feet wide. As I came near, I saw a huge rock on the other side. Standing next to the rock was a brilliant light being that I immediately recognized as a Christ Consciousness. The love, warmth, acceptance, and caring coming from that light were impossible to describe. Then a communication more than words spoke to me, saying: "As much as you love him, don't you know I love him more and I would never do anything that would

> really hurt him?" . . . Incidentally, my son is alive and well twenty-five years later.

Astounded, I phoned my friend to share, not *my* meadow experiences, but the report in Wolman's book. A secondhand mystical relay.

May's vision, a mother's encounter with Christ Consciousness, and conversations with a sidewalk artist and a church friend reassure me. I have nothing to fear. These people, as did I, experienced more than our minds could digest or our bodies attest. Yet vivid details linger, as does the knowledge that these mystical moments heal and fuel our lives.

Such narratives make me wonder. Is there a mystical landscape to be explored, not as a metaphor or archetypal myth, but as a spiritual reality? A common territory we know little about because we read the mystics but keep silent about our own soul journeys?

Catholic monk Wayne Teasdale, in his book *The Mystic Heart*, departs from centuries-old monastic teachings that instruct one to speak *from* mystical experiences but never *about* them. "Every one of us is a mystic," Teasdale writes. "We may or may not realize it; we may not even like it. But whether we know it or not, whether we accept it or not, mystical experience is always there, inviting us on a journey of ultimate discovery." Exchanging stories about such experiences and journeys, he believed, would foster an interfaith, global culture of shared spiritual values.

I am grateful for mystical moments and for journeys to landscapes beyond physical reality as we now know it. I am grateful to Linda and others who shared visions as they crossed over and for Brother Teasdale's encouragement to speak openly about such matters. But most of all, I am grateful for sacred meadows where the scent of roses sweetens the air and souls bask in inseparable and unending love.

Section Four

Repair My House

Assisi, Italy

Men shoulder machine guns in front of Francis's basilica while Clare's tomb stands unguarded. Few tourists venture beyond the city's walls to San Damiano where the saints' stories started. Sister Mary had insisted I go, so I trek the mile-long path, steep and strewn with white stones. Surrounded by olive trees, I imagine bandits and beasts Clare might have faced when she fled her home. A middle-aged man in a cleric's collar huffs his way toward me. Sweat streaks his face. We pause, greet one another. "Is it worth the hike back?" I ask. "Absolutely," he says and resumes his climb. Soon, I see the monastery's travertine blocks and plaster walls. Here, centuries ago, God spoke to Francis from a cross. Here, Clare turned away invading Saracens with prayer, nursed Francis in his last days. If they were to return, San Damiano is where they'd come.

in the sacred garden
deepening snow—still
a rose bush blooms

The Woman Whose Locks Francis Cut

"May God be with you always
and may you always be found in God."—*A Blessing of St. Clare*

Renouncing wealth to follow God's holy fool,
Clare fled through her home's death door.
As she died, the pope visited, sanctioned her Rule
which renounced wealth, like Francis, that holy fool.

Sainted in a mere two years, Clare left sisters who spooled
prayers, owned nothing, fasted while feeding the poor,
because she dared to follow Francis, God's holy fool,
fleeing wealth through her home's death door.

Monastery of St. Clare

Travelers Rest, South Carolina

Home from Assisi, I drive forty-five minutes down US Highway 25 to the Monastery of St. Clare. There, I park under a row of gleaming solar panels, walk past a small statue of Francis, and enter a womb-shaped chapel. Inside, sunlight beams through frosted squares onto a granite slab. Above it hangs a San Damiano cross. Sister Marie, wheelchair-bound, rolls to the lectern to read the psalms. Her voice rings strong. Here, thirteen cloistered nuns move in silence through each day, baking altar bread, weeding gardens, and mending their brown tunics. Sister Mary, who urged me to visit San Damiano, is among them. These women have prayed for me more than two decades. Today I will stroll the nature preserve across the road, recall Assisi's sweet olive blossoms as I breathe pine-scented air. Tonight, I will sleep at La Foresta, a retreat house with windowed walls.

brewing coffee
and chanting prayers . . .
dreams of lepers fade

On Retreat, St. Francis Springs

Stoneville, North Carolina

Driving in, we see grasses,
their golden lilt a welcome
in the autumn breeze

and believe
Francis would have smiled
to see us returning,

re-membering the circle
where we spin
stories of birth, death, rebirth.

We lumber in with baggage
we do not need,
check into our rooms,

settle into silence
like leaves greeting
forest floor.

Walking the Labyrinth

I enter a path with no false turns, no dead ends.
Under my feet, mica flecks dirt. Everything is stellar dust.

Stones curve toward petals where heaven descends.
I follow this path with no false turns, no dead ends,

stop to touch a sun-warmed rock, watch light bend.
My hands pulse   I am learning to trust

this path   no false turns   no dead ends
mica-flecked dirt   everything   nothing   but stellar dust.

Chasing the Mystery, One Labyrinth at a Time

Racing through a hotel in the 1990s, I spied a large white canvas stretched across a ballroom floor. For some strange reason, the concentric black circles stenciled on the cloth drew me like iron to a magnet. If I'd known then that entering that room would upend my world, I would've kept right on hoofing it down the hallway. But I didn't. Full of curiosity, I stopped and approached the information table to ask a woman with wiry brown hair if their program was part of the nonprofit conference I was attending.

"Yes, would you like to walk the labyrinth?"

"I'm not sure. I don't know what a labyrinth is."

"They've been around since before Roman times," she said, handing me a brochure that described how walking a labyrinth was one of the world's oldest contemplative practices.

"Wonder why I've never heard about them," I said, and, since her name tag bore the title Reverend, quickly added, "I've done centering prayer and *Lectio Divina*, but nothing like this."

"Not many people have. Dr. Lauren Artress, a priest at San Francisco's Grace Cathedral, first sparked my interest. They come in different shapes and sizes. The pattern here is a replica of the one in Chartres Cathedral. People walk them for all sorts of reasons—to reduce stress, ponder a question, pray for healing."

"Even to get a grant for their college?" I quipped. After all, *that* was why I was at the conference. "What if I get in and can't get back out?"

"You don't need to know anything about labyrinths before walking them," she reassured. "They're not like a maze. You can't get lost."

I didn't tell her, but I was already lost. My marriage was unraveling, and my children were struggling with their father's and my separation.

"This is probably not for me," I said in a last-ditch effort to resist the labyrinth's pull. "I'm in fundraising, not ministry."

"Everyone's in some kind of ministry," she replied.

If I'd left then, I could have caught the program about applying for grants that I'd been headed toward. Instead, I moved to the labyrinth's entrance, carrying worries on my back like a crammed knapsack. Once there, I slid off my heels and stepped onto the cloth that appeared larger than a wrestling mat.

The labyrinth's fabric felt cool under my feet. At first, I walked awkwardly, placing one foot in front of the other to stay within the designated lines. I was vaguely aware that a man was also walking the labyrinth, but as I rounded the circuits, my awareness of him faded, as did the burden of thoughts related to family and work. Any sense of time evaporated like a morning dew. Without knowing how I'd arrived there, I found myself in the labyrinth's center, a graphic shaped like a flower with six petals. There I heard the words: *Your work at the college is finished.*

Not "Get a divorce." Not "Call a family therapist." Not "Stay the course." Just, "*Your work at the college is finished.*"

Trembling, I scanned the room. Where had this message come from? There was no loudspeaker, no microphone, no burning bush. The woman at the table had her nose in a book. *That can't be*, I silently protested. I'd worked at the college for a decade and enjoyed what I did. The job was my financial security. My colleagues were like family.

I wanted to bolt across the cloth and out the door but instead carefully retraced my steps before finally exiting. The experience had left me reeling. I couldn't comprehend what had happened and I surely couldn't listen to any more conference presentations. I needed to get home and clear my head.

On the way back to my hotel room to pack, I bumped into the man who'd walked the path with me.

"You left the labyrinth in a hurry. Is anything wrong?" he asked.

"I don't know what happened in there, but I got a message I didn't need and don't want!"

He let my words resonate like a reverberating gong before speaking. "That's probably why you *should* pay attention. Was this your first labyrinth?"

"Yes," I said, putting my hands in my pockets to stop them from shaking.

"I've walked a few, and sometimes the experience can be unsettling."

As I drove home, the message I'd received rode beside me like an unwelcome hitchhiker. In the following days, I dismissed what had happened at the conference as nothing more than a product of my imagination. When that strategy didn't work, I rationalized my way out of the idea of leaving my job. After all, the message didn't actually say *quit your job*. Maybe it referred to one particular project. But in truth, nothing at work flowed as it had before. Easy tasks stalled. Coworkers feuded. One argument ended in a lawsuit where I feared being subpoenaed as a witness. The longer I stayed at the college, the more toxic the environment became.

It took me three years to resign. By then, my children were out of the house and the divorce finalized.

After leaving the college, I searched for labyrinths in various locations; but Dr. Artress' revival of this ancient practice was just gaining traction, and they were hard to find. When I did walk other labyrinths, nothing as dramatic occurred as what had happened at that conference.

In time, a different avenue of work opened for me: offering Circle of Trust® retreats based on a model pioneered by Parker J. Palmer. An educator and social activist, Parker's work with teachers, ministers, and healthcare providers galvanized my passion for empowering colleagues in ways that being a community college administrator had not. Ironically, I found myself in a ministry of sorts.

In my new work, I became an advocate for labyrinths, inviting retreat participants to walk them whenever venues offered one on-site. I also dragged friends to the local Methodist church when it unrolled its canvas at Easter and Christmas. Tonya, a woman I'd known since college, tolerated my constant urging but had her doubts. One day, to get me off her back, she agreed to visit a labyrinth, but only if I bought her lunch.

I checked a newly published online worldwide directory and discovered there was a labyrinth just a forty-five-minute drive away. The directions landed us in a field.

"You brought me all the way out here for *this*?" she asked as she exited the driver's seat of her SUV.

I confessed I too was a little surprised as we headed toward a circle of evenly spaced conical evergreens, each about five feet tall. The trees, perhaps planted to provide privacy, blocked our view of the path, but we soon found an opening that appeared to be the entrance.

"I'll be in and out in no time," Tonya announced as she stepped inside. If she'd asked a question or set an intention before entering, like I'd coached her to do, she never gave me the satisfaction of knowing.

I waited a few minutes before following her. I expected Tonya to rush through the circuits so she could search for four-leaf clovers, which she had an uncanny knack for finding, or head back to the car to check emails with the air conditioning running while I finished my rounds. But she was walking much slower than I'd imagined she would, and I quickly passed her. Twenty minutes later, I was the first to exit. I sat on a bench in the shade of a hickory to wait for her to finish. Ten more minutes passed. I wondered if I should walk the labyrinth again or call to her to make sure she was OK. The words *trust the process* flashed in my mind.

When Tonya did emerge, she ignored me and made a beeline to the car. There she opened the door, grabbed a pen, and scribbled notes on the back of a tattered grocery list.

"How long was I in there?" she finally asked.

"Just under an hour."

Tonya didn't tell me what happened, only that she'd received guidance about a matter which had been troubling her for years. As we rode home, she declared herself a believer.

One's first labyrinth is not unlike one's first love. After the initial meeting, each encounter holds its own gifts and surprises, in part because a person is different each time she steps inside. And every labyrinth that follows, like every new lover, offers a unique attraction. For those reasons, I approach a labyrinth I've never met by tuning my awareness to its pattern and surroundings. It could be a three-circuit path sheltered under a gazebo or five circuits mowed in a neighbor's lawn. Oaks may canopy a concrete pad that offers another replica of the twelve circuits I first walked. Less often, I embark on a Cretan pattern, whose seven circuits resemble a brain. This design dates back to 2000 BCE, long before Christians trudged designs on cathedral floors in lieu of pilgrimages to the Holy Land.

No matter the design or size, the three-part movement of walking a labyrinth remains the same: first, entering with a focus or question, then surrendering to the power of the moment as one walks and rests in the center, and finally, giving thanks as one exits. Watches, cell phones, and pressing commitments are best left outside.

I've seen people skip, dance, stride, and even sit down while navigating a labyrinth. When outdoors, dry leaves crunching underfoot or the sight of a cardinal feeding his mate might draw one's attention. Inside, light may stream through stained-glass windows, rainbowing floors and walls. Sometimes, as a person circumambulates, a new focus arises. If so, the counsel is to listen, as Saint Benedict taught, with the ear of the heart.

As a person makes this inner and outer journey, one's body can enter a state of quiet equilibrium. It can also become a divining rod, vibrating signals and transmitting messages between Earth and sky. There's no way to predict what might arise. An enemy's face may float before one's eyes. The line of a poem suddenly land on one's tongue.

Becoming aware of when it's time to leave is much like waking from a dream. One's vision changes as blurred bricks or a fuzzy altar come into focus. A foot may cramp or cheeks start to smart due to a cold breeze. Retracing the path, one returns to chronological time and three-dimensional forms with a bit of the mystery still clinging.

As more people discovered labyrinths, they began appearing in public parks, forests, and playgrounds. Their energy felt familiar, much like friends but with different gifts, until I discovered one whose location, size, and shape had been created using an ancient art known as dowsing. Traditionally practiced in the Blue Ridge Mountains primarily to locate water underground, dowsing engages the body in a form of kinesthetic listening.

The discovery took place on a Sunday afternoon. Jaan Ferree, a member of my women's group, and I were at a housewarming party for a mutual friend. The celebration included walking a serpentine path that meandered through a mini-forest in the side yard. Prayer flags, inspirational quotes, and chimes festooned its twists and turns. A small bench waited in the center. Weaving in the shade of dogwoods and oaks, my body warmed as if I were in a sauna.

"I've constructed a lot of labyrinths," Jaan shared after we'd finished our walk, "but when Jerene told me she wanted one here, at her home, I knew I would dowse for it."

Will Rockingbear, a Cherokee elder, had first introduced Jaan to labyrinths outside his lodge in Burnsville, North Carolina. Intrigued, she'd enrolled in Dr. Artress' labyrinth facilitator training in the early 2000s. But it was Marty Cain, a Boston-based sculptor, who'd taught Jaan how to dowse for them.

Years before the two women met, Marty had been invited to create a temporary art installation at Harvard University. Employing techniques that she'd learned when she was a child from her Lithuanian grandfather, she'd dowsed and constructed a labyrinth on the university's green. I was struck later, watching a YouTube video, how Marty laughed as she recalled the scene. "It was during finals, and nobody knew what a labyrinth was. Students poured out of the dorms at all hours of the night to walk it."

After learning the art from Marty, Jaan dowsed half a dozen labyrinths before laying out the path in our friend's yard. Those projects included one for a horticulture symposium at Davidson College, another for a therapeutic riding program in Highlands, North Carolina, and a three-circuit Zen garden which served as a meditation site at Valle Crucis Conference Center until a flood washed the pattern away.

"That one in Highlands," she said, "was large enough for horses to enter. In fact, a horse followed me the whole time I was dowsing."

Jaan uses two rods shaped like L's when she works. "They're like wearing a pair of glasses or a hearing aid. They help me sense and feel what energy I'm picking up."

Before beginning, she smudges herself to clear personal emotions so that she's energetically clean. Then she makes an offering of cornmeal or tobacco to the land, the spirits of the land, the elementals, and the ancestors. Only then does she ask for help and pose the question: Is there a labyrinth here? If the rods point outward, indicating "Yes," she asks to be shown its center, entrance, and outer rim framed by the cardinal directions. As these are revealed, she marks the exterior boundaries and the interior spiraling path with surveyors' flags and tape. These markers serve as guides for where to install bricks, tiles, or stones.

Eager to learn more about the body's role as an antenna for Earth's energy, I asked if I could watch the next time she dowsed for a labyrinth. Jaan had shared that she usually worked alone to eliminate any static that might interfere with her ability to receive signals. I was grateful when she agreed to let me join her.

My opportunity to observe came on a late fall afternoon. Jaan carried her rods as we entered a grove of pines near a park in Flat Rock, North Carolina. Her red jacket flapped in the wind. A new church was planned for this property, and members wanted to construct a labyrinth. They'd asked her to tell them where it should be located.

First Jaan extracted a bundle of sage, lit it, and with the smoke smudged herself, the rods, and me. I then stood at a distance and watched as she made her offerings, called in ancestors and guides for the afternoon's work, and posed the question, "Is there a labyrinth here on this property?"

The rods did not move.

Jaan walked to another location and posed the same questions. Still the rods did not move.

Surprised at the lack of a response, she tried one other site before conceding.

"Do you think my being here has anything to do with your not getting an answer?" I asked.

"It's not you," she said. "I seldom get a 'No,' but when I do, I don't force it. It would be disrespectful to build a labyrinth on this land when there's not one here."

I was disappointed at not being able to witness the process, but as Jaan packed up to leave, she shared a deeper yearning. "We need to listen more to Earth's guidance, and labyrinths aren't the only way. People from indigenous cultures walk energy grids without surface patterns all the time. When we go shoeless, the soles of our feet can pick up clues, and our bodies can become dowsing rods."

Jaan's words about listening with our feet were not entirely foreign to me. Growing up in South Georgia, I went barefoot from the day school let out in May until it resumed in September. Despite occasionally stepping on a nail, which required a kerosene foot-soaking, or picking out a raft of sand spurs lodged in my heels, I relished silky sand and sucking mud between my toes.

But it wasn't until I'd hiked in a redwood forest that I felt nudged to explore the potential of my body as an energetic antenna. On one of the trails, I passed a massive clearing where a mother tree had died and left a ring of progeny. Wood sorrel, salmonberry, and western sword fern blanketed the ground. I stepped off the marked path and onto the forest floor. Silence as thick as fog surrounded me. I challenged myself: could I attune to Earth's elements enough to receive clues, to walk a path not etched in concrete or outlined with bricks, pebbles, or bushes?

Feeling foolish (I didn't think I had those kinds of gifts) and skeptical (nothing's going to happen), I walked into the shadow of those giant beings. Admiring the coastal sequoias was one thing. Thinking I'd be guided among them was another.

That's when the buzzing started. My body listed to the left, so I stepped in that direction. I stood still until I felt another tug, this time pulling me forward. Responding to that invisible communiqué was like feeling my way down an unlit path, but subsequent moves seemed directed by physical cues like a V-shaped branch, a scrub jay's call prompting me to turn, a cairn stacked by a previous hiker.

I couldn't visualize what kind of pattern my footsteps were forming, nor did I care. My feet were learning to read Earth's braille as my heart opened to the unfolding mystery. I glided into what seemed to be the center of a sacred vortex and there experienced a lightness of being. Perhaps this was the place where the mother tree had once flourished. Or perhaps a stream of water flowed beneath its surface. But as suddenly as the guidance had appeared, it departed.

My experiment had ended, but the wonder lingered. And although I've yet to learn how to dowse, and my "Earthspeak" vocabulary is that of a two-year-old, I've come to hold everything as holy. I frequently take off my shoes.

During the pandemic, my physical body and spiritual journey became closely wedded when I underwent open-heart surgery. After months of being unable to hike or garden, and dependent upon others for the most minor of tasks, I felt called again to seek out the wisdom of a labyrinth. And not just any labyrinth, but one I'd never walked before. My friend Tonya, ever on the lookout, suggested I try a newly constructed path at Holmes Educational State Forest near Hendersonville, North Carolina.

As I crossed the lawn toward the labyrinth, three young children, siblings under the age of six, zigzagged in front of me. They jumped over stones, spun in circles, and called to their grandmother to watch their next moves.

"We'll be leaving soon," she said, addressing herself to me. "I know you're here for some quiet meditation."

"There's no hurry," I said. "It's refreshing to be around such enthusiasm."

I'd come there that day agitated with questions about my future. When would my physical energy return? Should I move into a retirement community to better age in place? How should I use what time I had left? The youngsters' laughter had called me out of my head and into my heart.

After the children left, I approached the labyrinth with a new focus. The surgery had granted me an encore. Whatever days I had remaining, I wanted to play an airy, cheerful tune, one that would echo the afternoon's breezy sunshine and the children's good-natured humor.

I stepped inside a space that was now a trusted friend, rounded the first curve, then paused to pray and listen. That's when I heard another message. This time it wasn't words. It was bluebirds, and whispering trees, and the sounds of water in a nearby creek. They were singing. And they were singing for me.

Section Five

After Compline

Montreat, North Carolina

Looking at the lake, I might have missed
a gibbous moon ghosting the limbs
of short-needled pines but your face

on the bridge, silvered and upturned,
drew mine, would not let me miss
such borrowed light on its nightly round.

We stood there hushed.   After a time
I walked toward home not having missed
that gibbous moon, those ghosted limbs.

Ushered

In the wind-chilled North
where White Buffalo and majestic Oak reign
where Hummingbird ferries
prayers to spirit guides and green streaks
singed with purple fringe
float in luminous skies

a door appears
through which souls enter this world of form
then return

a threshold guarded by Ancient Ones
who monitor the comings
the goings
so perilous the passage

and we, clouded by unknowing,
find ourselves ushered forth
and back, back and forth,
clothing in a body for each arrival
disrobing to rest.

It is not ours to touch
the how, the why
but here in the somewhere
we are sometimes blessed
with a glimpse of others crossing—
the door ajar at births,
during deaths, in our dreams.

if there are other lifetimes

let me come back as music—
notes floating above a silver flute, breath
passing through an oboe's quavering reeds—

not as howling wind or a lion's growl,
not even as crackling fire
or booming waves

but as a tune that cheers a village dance
or a melody that lulls
a child to sleep.

A Litany for Ancestor Wisdom

In a world divorced
from knowledge that cannot be
    parsed or proved

    a world where cities burn
        and politicians harden lines

make us porous

so we can commune
    with cedars
        receive messages
            from sprites
                and saints
    and spiral like galaxies.

In a time when the old squander
and the young
    have no use for prattle,

open us to ancestor wisdom
    not how to lard
        bank accounts
            or smash ceilings

but how to dance in evil's shadow.

In an age of rising seas
        and cracked deserts
expand our living
        beyond gated pettiness.

Quench our fears enough to share
        a cup of tea,
        a slice of bread.

Reading Rilke in Early Morning Light

"My blood is alive with many voices
telling me I am made of longing."—*Rainer Maria Rilke*

His words, as lustrous and tart on the tongue
as communion wine, wash over
my body, lift me on a tide that surges
past ages and nations. Wind crests waves,

waves caress galaxies in a universe of endless
shorelines, and I marvel at the travel underway—
the zigzags, spirals and swarms. Horizons
dissolve as cities groan. The solid ground

I once stood upon now glitters
quicksand. In the surround, a honeyed
ache of separation. And those voices,
that longing, urge me on

a starved lover returning
light to star, salt to sea.

I Want It Said of Me, As It Was of Him

"In his last days, he leaked light . . ."
—*Barbara Brown Taylor*, eulogy for the Rt. Rev. Bennett J. Sims

I want it said, in my old age, that I leak light.
With every wrinkle, I grow brighter; with every ache,
the dandelion becomes my guide.

I'm not talking about leaks that arrive unwelcomed. A shower
that sputters, only to settle into syncopated plops. Headlines
that risk national security. Heart valves that spill with each pump.

A busted pipe undetected for hours flooded a friend's home
before setting off alarms. Water can be like that. But light?

Today I want to speak of how it flames in a hearth, glistens
from melting snow. How when so much shines from a body
toward the end of life, it gilds everyone in its flow.

Mikvah

The first time I encountered the word *mikvah* was while reading an Anne Rice book, not one of her vampire tales, but her novel *Christ the Lord*, which she wrote after returning to Catholicism. I can't recall the scene. It could have been Mary bathing in a mikvah after Jesus' birth. Perhaps it was another female character purifying herself seven days following her menses. I do remember the connection Rice made between immersion in a mikvah, a consecrated pool of water, and the Christian rite of baptism.

The memory of reading that word faded until David and Elissa, Jewish friends I'd known since college, were helping me sort out my life. We were sitting on my back porch in the late afternoon gloam, glasses of red wine in our hands. Several months earlier, I'd buried my father. I'd taken care of him for five years after my mother died. Clearing out the home they'd built and loved for half a century triggered unresolved grief over my marriage's end a decade before.

There, in the backyard with these friends looking on, I'd ritually burned a stack of letters from my former husband. I don't know why I'd kept those missives, perhaps for our children. David and Elissa had introduced us, so it was fitting they witnessed that closing act. I needed to put that chapter of my life behind. I planned to leave in a few weeks on a pilgrimage to see the giant Sequoias and coastal redwoods, a trip I'd postponed until after my father's death, and one I'd looked forward to all my life.

Elissa, who as long as we'd known each other could almost read my mind, sensed my struggle. "If you were Jewish," she said, "I'd tell you to find a mikvah and offer what you're hanging on to as a sacrifice. In Judaism, we have a saying: 'What freed you from bondage cannot see you into the promised land.'"

"There are times, Elissa, when I wish I were Jewish."

A few days later, I had lunch with my friend Jaan, who'd introduced me to labyrinths.

"I need a ceremony to free me of this overwhelming grief and invite in more joy," I told her as we munched on salads and chips. I then proceeded to describe my conversation with Elissa about the mikvah ritual.

"That's interesting," she said. "Native Americans also have traditions that include immersing themselves in running water. Why don't you create your own ritual—a rebirthing ceremony of sorts?"

"I never thought of that," I said, my face likely looking as puzzled as someone who'd just been spoken to in a language they didn't understand.

"On your trip," she advised, "look for a creek or stream in the forest where you can be alone. Dip yourself seven times to honor the cardinal directions, Mother Earth, Father Sky, and the Mystery within."

As we got up from our table to part, she added, "And don't forget to ask for what you need."

I used to speak lightly of fate or synchronicity, but the ensuing trip through California and Oregon made me a believer in both. For four days, as I hiked in ancient forests among towering sequoias, Western redwoods, and Douglas fir, I searched for running water. I saw creeks I could have waded in, but never found one hidden and deep enough to strip my clothes off, immerse myself, and offer the prayers I needed.

I'll find a place for the ritual when I'm back in the Blue Ridge Mountains, I consoled myself as I pulled into Jackson Wellsprings in Ashland, Oregon, to visit the public spa there. It was a Sunday afternoon and a Peace Festival was underway. People from different religious traditions and pagan practices were camping in tents, grilling near RVs, drumming, droning, and dancing a little too ecstatically for me after the quiet solitude I'd enjoyed. Feeling out of place, I soon decided to leave.

That's when I noticed a poster on an outdoor announcement board. *Mikvah: Call to schedule.*

Could this be real? I wondered as I entered the office to inquire. Stevie, a woman with dark cropped hair, greeted me from behind the counter.

"Yes, there's a ceremonial pool here on the property," she said. "I can show it to you if you'd like."

"I'd appreciate that."

The path we followed, one which mercifully led away from the noise of the festivities, passed a Goddess temple, forded a small stream, then switchbacked through woods toward an enclosure about the size of a tiny house. There was no roof. Tree branches reached through its cedar walls like welcoming arms. Here I could see the sky and still have the privacy I needed to soak unobserved.

"The mikvah was built in 2010," Stevie told me as we stepped inside. "When the rabbis consecrated it, they poured water from the Himalayas, India, and Israel into the pool."

"So it's not just for Jewish people?" I asked.

"Oh, no. We've had Christians, Sufis, and Buddhists hold ceremonies here. People passing through sometimes fill up a bottle and take it to other sacred sites they love."

I glanced around, taking in the medicinal herbs planted nearby and a small altar with a statue of a deity I couldn't identify.

"I was told the water should be flowing."

"See that opening in the rock?" she said, pointing to a shelf behind me. "That's where springs feed into the pool. Whenever we have groups like this weekend, staff members guard this place so it won't be desecrated."

"I'd like to reserve a time but not while the festival is underway."

"Most people will leave tomorrow."

I booked an hour slot on Tuesday. Extending my stay would give me a day to prepare.

The idolatrous proposition of creating a rebirthing ritual that I would preside over for myself still felt unnerving to me. When I was a child, an ordained minister baptized me in Coochie Creek, a few miles outside the town where I grew up in rural Georgia. I can still recall the swirling brown water and how fish nibbled my legs as he invoked, "*In the name of the Father and the Son and the Holy Ghost . . .*"

In my twenties and thirties, firmly embedded as I was in the Christian story, the practice of communing directly with water and sky, and inviting guides, protectors, and ancestors to accompany me in ritual, was not in my repertoire. Not until author and teacher John Philip Newell introduced me to Celtic Christianity did I have a framework for God in all things and all things in God.

As for the disrobing required for immersion in a mikvah, the only time I'd ever skinny-dipped was in my sister's pool during the time I was looking after my father. I'd been hiring caregivers, driving him to medical appointments, and helping with finances. I could see dementia clouding his mind. Yet, knowing that he couldn't process information didn't lessen the sting when he accused me of stealing.

"My own daughter," he said. "I can't believe you'd do that to me."

"Who *do* you trust?" I asked, hoping to calm his distress.

When he named his accountant, I grabbed the opportunity to turn over the checkbooks and cleansed myself of his accusation by swimming nude. My behavior was so out of character that when my sister spied me from her utility room window, she came running to see what was wrong. Perhaps that shedding and immersion was a kind of prelude to this occasion. I was here to rid myself not only of clothing but of lingering grief, overgrown responsibilities, and outworn preconceptions.

That hour on a Tuesday morning at the mikvah in Jackson Wellsprings proved to be more dreamlike than real, what spiritual seekers deem a kairos experience. The notes in my journal, along with an ongoing awareness of having been blessed during that time, serve as witness to what happened there. And like a dream, if I try hard enough, I can even recall the scenes.

The grounds are eerily quiet when I stop by the office to pick up the key. I retrace my steps through the woods and take a deep breath as I unlock the mikvah's door. A catch in my throat alerts me that even though I need to be here, I am still uncertain how to proceed. I circle the glistening pool surrounded by rock terraces; seven steps lead into water about four feet deep. Despite my having crafted a ceremony, this is new territory for me. I pause and pray for guidance. As if in response, the water refracts sunlight beaming through overhanging trees, not quite a kaleidoscope effect, but a show just the same. Dragonflies swarm cattails planted near the fence.

That's when I know the pink bathing suit beneath my sky-blue cover-up has to go. I walk to the dressing area to leave my journal, cell phone, and clothes. If I am opening to rebirth, no books, technology, or fabric can come between me and the water.

Returning to the pool's side, albeit self-conscious in my birthday suit, I offer an opening prayer that this ceremony cleanse me of past fears and doubts and usher in new life. The air silks my skin. I dip my toes into water the temperature of a tepid bath. When I plant my foot on the first step, there is no turning back.

Descending into the water triggers memories of a past dream. I'm traveling through underground tunnels to my grandmother's grave, a location I've kept secret in the dream for years. Another tunnel leads to a space below her tomb where I've never ventured. I follow that tunnel and end beside a pool. It is there that Christ appears and baptizes me, not in water but in a woman's blood.

On this day, however, I am outside and not underground. I am sixty-five, not in my forties as when I had that dream. There is no priest, no rabbi, no grandmother's crypt. Instead of human blood, there is the sap of life. In this moment I am the child who hungered for communion, the woman who fled a marriage to search for healing; I am the daughter now orphaned. I stand in a pool up to my neck, ready for death, rebirth, and new life. It is time to begin.

To honor my Jewish friends and their tradition, I submerge myself three times. After each, I offer a prayer and ask, even though I can't articulate exactly what I need, to be open to receive.

Next, I turn in each of the seven directions, offer thanks for its gifts, lower myself into the water, and rise like a dolphin breaching the sea. At the end, I shake my hair free of water and pound my ears to clear them.

Finally, I raise my right arm to the open sky, blue as a peacock's feather, like I recall that preacher doing in Coochie Creek, and utter baptismal words that are truer to who I am now: *In the name of the Creator, Lover, and Sustainer.* I tilt backwards, a trust fall into the sacred water, then pull myself up, dripping.

Feeling spent and sensing the ritual complete, I float on my back, naked as a newborn. A host of butterflies, golden in the light, dance above my face.

Notes

Epigraph—These lines are taken from the poem "Hide and Seek" in *Love Nailed to the Doorpost* by Richard Chess, 2017, p. 60.

SECTION ONE

As a Child—This and four other poems in the collection are haibun, a form popularized in the seventeenth century by Japanese poet Bashō which combines a prose poem with a haiku. The narrative is often about a journey. The haiku provides an imagistic reflection grounded in nature, alludes to a season, and contains a shift or turn. For more information, read Aimee Nezhukumatahil's essay "More than the Birds, Bees, and Trees: A Closer Look at Writing Haibun" at the Academy of American Poets' website.

You First—Julian of Norwich (1342–c. 1416) is the name given to an anchoress who lived at St. Julian's Church in Norwich, England, during the bubonic plague. She is believed to have been the first woman to write a book in English that has survived. In *Revelations of Divine Love*, Julian recounts visions she received on May 8, 1373, when she thought she was dying. Teresa of Ávila (1515–82), a Discalced Carmelite nun, mystic, poet, and religious reformer, survived the Spanish Inquisition and was named a Doctor of the Church in 1970. Her book *The Interior Castle* describes the soul's inner journey through seven levels until reaching mystical union with God. Hildegard of Bingen (1098–1179), a Benedictine abbess, herbalist, and composer, traveled and preached in Germany, where she often challenged church and political leaders. Perhaps that's why it was not until 2012 that she was canonized and elevated to a Doctor of the Church, one of only four women along with Teresa to hold that honor. Hildegard recorded her visions, wrote numerous treatises on saints, medicine, and natural history, and set her lyric poems to music. Mirabai Starr has written extensively about Julian, Teresa, Hildegard, and other women mystics in *Wild Mercy: Living the Fierce and Tender Wisdom of the Women Mystics*. She has also translated *The Interior Castle* and *Revelations of Divine Love* for contemporary readers. Another excellent resource is Abbey of the Arts, an online monastery whose abbess Christine Valters Paintner has written extensively about both men and women mystics. Her book *Illuminating the Way: Embracing the Wisdom of Monks and Mystics* has a chapter devoted to Hildegard.

The Word—In 2 Corinthians 12:2–4, Paul writes, "I knew a man in Christ . . . caught up to the third heaven. And I knew such a man (whether in the body, or out of the body, I cannot tell: God knoweth); How that he was caught up into paradise, and heard unspeakable words, which it is not lawful for a man to utter" (KJV). I remember quizzing a lay preacher about out-of-body experiences when I was a teen. In response, he quoted the above verses.

Adrift—The epigraph is from Annie Dillard's "An Expedition to the Pole" found in *The Annie Dillard Reader*, 1995, p. 31. Dreams are termed lucid when one is asleep and is aware one is dreaming. Sometimes the dreamer can become an active participant. It can also be like watching a movie in one's sleep.

SECTION TWO

Who Believes a Woman's Tale—Mary Magdalene, or Mary the Tower (the name Magdala means tower in Aramaic), has been a controversial and elusive figure dating back to early Christianity. At the 2022 Wild Goose Festival, Diana Butler Bass delivered a sermon titled "All the Marys," which explored the mystery of who Mary was, details of her Christological confession in John 11 (previously thought to be spoken by Martha), as well as her proclamation of the resurrection. This sermon went viral, sparking interest in Elizabeth Schrader Polczer's groundbreaking research, the basis for Bass' sermon. For more information, read or listen to Amy Frykholm's interview of Bass in *The Christian Century*'s *In Search Of* podcast, February 14, 2024, or go to Bass' website. Beth Maczka, to whom this poem is dedicated, brought this information to my attention. Her research, yet to be published, focuses on Mary Magdalene's role as the unnamed anointer of Jesus in Mark 14:3–9, following which Jesus proclaims, "What she has done will be told in remembrance of her."

St. Columba's Isle—In 563 CE, St. Columba (c. 521–97), an Irish priest and missionary monk, sailed from Ireland in a coracle (a small boat with a wooden or wicker frame and, legend has it, no anchor or oars) with twelve disciples to establish a religious community on Iona in Scotland. The tiny island off the southwest coast of Mull in the Inner Hebrides became a sacred place where Scottish, Irish, and Norwegian kings were buried. Repeated attacks by Viking raiders in the early 800s led the monks to relocate to an abbey in Ireland. In 1938, the Rev. George MacLeod established the Iona Community, an ecumenical religious community comprised of laypersons and clergy to carry on the spirit of Columba's mission. For rich stories about the island, regarded as Scotland's "Cradle of Christianity" and home to the Celtic tradition, read John Philip Newell's *Listening for the Heartbeat of God: A Celtic Spirituality*, his chapter about George MacLeod in *Sacred Earth, Sacred Soil: Celtic Wisdom for Reawakening to What Our Souls*

Know and Healing the World, or visit websites maintained by the Iona Community Council and the National Trust for Scotland.

Above the Atlantic—At St. Columba's Bay, visitors often collect rainbow-colored stones. Especially prized are small, teardrop-shaped pebbles with streaks of translucent green called Columba's Tears or Mermaid's Tears. My guide shared the legend that carrying one of these pebbles in one's pocket protects the person from drowning. Britta Schmitz's post in Findhorn Foundation's newsletter offers more information along with beautiful photographs of these stones.

In a Parallel Life—An Italian saint, Clare of Assisi (1194–1253), was one of the first followers of Saint Francis of Assisi and founded the Order of Poor Ladies, now known as Poor Clares. Bret Thoman, OFS, chronicles her journey in *St. Clare of Assisi: Light from the Cloister.* Brigid of Kildare (451–525), who earlier in her life was a slave and bears the name of a Celtic goddess, is the mother saint of Ireland. She founded a monastery called the Church of the Oak (*Cill Dara*, or Kildare) beneath a large tree on the site of a pagan shrine. In *Sacred Earth, Sacred Soul*, John Philip Newell chose Brigid as his model of the sacred feminine. Christine Valters Paintner in *Illuminating the Way* focuses on her healing ministry. Both authors point to the support between men and women saints as evidenced by the friendship and mutual respect between Brigid and Patrick and Clare and Francis.

New Bearings: A Jubilee Pilgrimage to Iona—Mark Nepo's poem, a portion of which is used as the epigraph, can be found in *The Book of Awakening: Having the Life You Want by Being Present to the Life You Have*, 2000, p. 34. Before going on my Iona pilgrimage, I had the privilege of meeting the Rev. Douglas C. Vest, whose book *On Pilgrimage* became a guide for my journey. For additional information about Columba, Iona, and Celtic Christianity, read John Philip Newell's book *Listening to the Heartbeat of God: A Celtic Spirituality* or visit Iona's websites.

SECTION THREE

Frozen Music—The twelfth century witnessed a transition from Romanesque architecture with dark rounded arches and tunnel vaults to the Gothic style, an elegant combination of geometrical patterns including pointed arches, vaulted ceilings, and rose windows. Most Cistercian churches built in that century were plain and unadorned, but some adopted features of the Gothic cathedrals, especially the pointed arch. For a comprehensive exploration of this transition, along with stunning photographs, visit Rost Architecture Interiors' website post "The History of Gothic Cathedrals: The Architecture of Light."

Noon Prayer in Salisbury Cathedral—Salisbury Cathedral, formally the Cathedral Church of the Blessed Virgin Mary, is an Anglican site of worship in Salisbury, England. Built between 1220 and 1258, a relatively short period of 38 years, its tower and spire were not completed until 1330. From 1986 until 2023, the cathedral underwent major renovations. Surrounded by cloisters, the cathedral is constructed in the shape of a double cross. Salisbury Plain, a 300-square-mile chalk plateau in Southern England is famous for its history and archeology, including rings of standing stones, the most famous of which is Stonehenge. The Cathedral maintains a website which includes a history of the cathedral and information about its museum, which has one of the four surviving original Magna Cartas from 1215. Edward Rutherfurd's historical novel *Sarum*, which follows five families from the Ice Age to the twentieth century, includes the building of Stonehenge and, thirty-two centuries later, of the cathedral at New Sarum.

Winter Lights—Mark Stephen Burrows' poem "Nine Forms of Light" inspired this poem and can be found in his collection *The Chance of Home.*

Sacred Meadows—This essay underwent many revisions. Each time I thought it was complete, someone I knew would share another experience or I would read a new account of a mystical meadow. The ones from printed sources that I included are Jim Robbins' *The Man Who Planted Trees*, 2015, p. 79; Gerald May's "Angels at the Edge," from *Shalem News*, fall of 1995; Richard N. Wolman's *Thinking with Your Soul: Spiritual Intelligence and Why It Matters*, 2001, p. 130; and Wayne Teasdale's *The Mystic Heart: Discovering a Universal Spirituality in the World's Religions*, 2001, p. 3. The epigraph is taken from Robert Duncan's poem "Often I Am Permitted to Return to a Meadow." The full poem can be found on The Poetry Foundation's website.

SECTION FOUR

Repair My House—St. Francis of Assisi (1181–1230) was an Italian Catholic friar who founded the Order of Lesser Brothers, or "Little Brothers," with an emphasis on humility and a life of poverty. The basilica to honor him was built inside the walled city, but it was outside the city, in the abandoned San Damiano church, where Francis heard a voice speak from a Byzantine crucifix: "Go, and rebuild my house which, as you can see, is totally in ruin" (Bret Thoman, *St. Francis of Assisi: Passion, Poverty, and the Man Who Transformed the Catholic Church*, 2018, p. 66). Francis toiled to restore the dilapidated building, and, in 1212, San Damiano became home to Clare and her growing order. Only in hindsight did the mission of restoring the greater Catholic Church become clear, a topic explored by Richard Rohr in *Eager to Love: The Alternative Way of Francis of Assisi*. Today San Damiano belongs to the Friars Minor. The cross from which Francis heard a voice was moved to the Basilica of Saint Clare. A replica hangs in its place. The convent garden, where Francis composed his "Canticle of the Creatures," is where legend has it that Francis, leaving barefoot in the snow, told Clare he would visit her again when the roses bloomed. A bush immediately flowered. Clare cut a bouquet and put it under the crucifix in the dormitory where she and her sisters slept. The Assisi Project recounts the story in "The Legend of the Winter Roses" on their website. Francis's "Canticle" can be found in *The St. Clare Prayer Book: Listening for God's Leading* by Jon M. Sweeney.

The Woman Whose Locks Francis Cut—Clare, the daughter of a noble family, heard Francis preach in 1210 and felt God calling her to a life of penance and poverty. On Palm Sunday in 1212, she left through her home's death door, an opening in medieval houses used to remove bodies, and met Francis in a small chapel called Our Lady of the Angels. There she was tonsured and received the coarse habit. Clare lived briefly with Benedictine Sisters before moving to San Damiano, where she remained cloistered the remainder of her life. Clare rejected rules the Church tried to impose on her order, insisting that she and her sisters be granted the privilege of radical poverty that Francis espoused. In 1247, Clare began writing her own Rule of Life, the first woman to do so. Pope Innocent IV approved it two days before she died. For more of her story, read *St. Clare of Assisi: Light from the Cloister* by Bret Thoman, OFS, or *In the Footsteps of Francis and Clare* by Roch Niemier, OFM. The epigraph is a prayer that South Carolina Poor Clare Sisters sent me forth with after I facilitated a discernment process about whether they were to build a new monastery. The words appear on cards sold on their website as a part of their ministry. Jon Sweeney offers more of Clare and Francis' prayers in *The St. Clare Prayer Book: Listening for God's Leading.*

Monastery of St. Clare, Travelers Rest—Riding his horse outside of Assisi, Francis met a man afflicted with leprosy. Although Francis was horrified and disgusted, he dismounted his horse, embraced, and kissed him. Toward the end of his life, Francis wrote that meeting this leper marked the beginning of his conversion. A chapter is devoted to the encounter in Bret Thoman's book about St. Francis. For information about the monastery, visit the sisters' website.

On Retreat, St. Francis Springs—According to its website, St. Francis Springs Prayer Center is inspired by the charism (spiritual gifts) of St. Francis and St. Clare. The vision of Father Louis Canino, the North Carolina retreat center honors nature's beauty, offers a place for deep contemplation grounded in God's love, promotes justice and peace, and excels in Franciscan hospitality. I was privileged to colead Circle of Trust® retreats there with John Fenner. To learn more about these retreats, which grew out of the work and writing of Parker J. Palmer, visit the website for the Center for Courage & Renewal.

Chasing the Mystery, One Labyrinth at a Time—In 1996, Lauren Artress founded the nonprofit Veriditas, a worldwide project to "pepper the planet with labyrinths." More about that work, including information about upcoming pilgrimages, can be found at laurenartress.com and veriditas.org. To watch the YouTube video in which Melinda Iverson Inn interviews Marty Cain, go to *Wisdom Keepers of Earth*, "Dowsing Sacred Labyrinths: Marty Cain in Conversation with Melinda," posted April 21, 2022.

SECTION FIVE

After Compline—Compline, also known as Night Prayer, is a Christian service which takes place at day's end. The word comes from the Latin word *completorium*, meaning completion. The tradition of saying or singing Compline dates back to at least the sixth century. The end of the service marks the beginning of the Great Silence, during which monks and nuns do not speak until the first service of the following day. Various resources for this service can be found online, including the Cathedral Music Trust's "Compline in a Nutshell."

Reading Rilke in Early Morning Light—The epigraph comes from *Rilke's Book of Hours: Love Poems to God*, 2005, translated by Anita Barrows and Joanna Macy. The lines can be found in the first section, *The Book of a Monastic Life*, 2005, p. 99.

I Want It Said of Me, As It Was of Him—The Rt. Rev. Bennett Sims was an Episcopal priest who served as the bishop of the Diocese of Atlanta. Deeply influenced by Quaker Robert Greenleaf, Sims founded the Institute for Servant Leadership at Emory's Candler School of Theology, where he taught. After retirement, he and his wife Mary Page moved to Flat Rock, North Carolina, and hosted a house church. I worshiped there for more than a decade. Sims authored several books including *Servanthood: Leadership for the Third Millenium*. Barbara Brown Taylor, also an Episcopal priest and one of Sims' students, is known for her thought-provoking books, including *Leaving Church: A Memoir of Faith*, *Altar in the World: A Geography of Faith*, and *Holy Envy: Finding God in the Faith of Others*.

Bibliography

Abbey of the Arts. "A Virtual Monastery and Global Community." https://abbeyofthearts.com/.

Artress, Lauren. "A Leading Force in the Modern Labyrinth Movement." https://laurenartress.com/.

The Assisi Project. "The Legend of the Winter Roses." January 15, 2020. https://assisiproject.com/2020/01/15/the-legend-of-the-winter-roses-2/.

Bass, Diana Butler. "All the Marys: Wild Goose Festival Closing Sermon, July 17, 2022." https://dianabutlerbass.com/wp-content/uploads/2023/06/Mary-the-Tower.pdf.

Burrows, Mark Stephen. "Nine Forms of Light." In *The Chance of Home*, 96–98. Brewster, MA: Paraclete, 2018.

Cathedral Music Trust. "Compline in a Nutshell." https://www.cathedralmusictrust.org.uk/discover/compline-in-a-nutshell/.

Chess, Richard. "Hide and Seek." In *Love Nailed to the Doorpost*, 59–60. Tampa, FL: University of Tampa Press, 2017.

Center for Courage & Renewal. "Parker J. Palmer." https://couragerenewal.org/parker-j-palmer/.

Dillard, Annie. "An Expedition to the Pole." In *The Annie Dillard Reader*, 20–47. New York: Harper Perennial, 1995.

Duncan, Robert. "Often I Am Permitted to Return to a Meadow." The Poetry Foundation. https://www.poetryfoundation.org/poems/46317/often-i-am-permitted-to-return-to-a-meadow.

Frykholm, Amy. "There's Something About Mary Magdalene, with Elizabeth Schrader Polczer and Diana Butler Bass (S3:E1)." Produced by *The Christian Century. In Search Of*, February 14, 2024. Podcast, MP3 audio. https://www.christiancentury.org/there-s-something-about-mary-magdalene-elizabeth-schrader-polczer-and-diana-butler-bass-s3-e1.

Inn, Melinda Iverson. "Dowsing Sacred Labyrinths: Marty Cain in Conversation with Melinda." *Wisdom Keepers of Earth*, April 21, 2022. Podcast, video. https://melindaiversoninn.com/dowsing-sacred-labyrinths-with-marty-cain/.

Isle of Iona. "Isle of Iona." http://www.welcometoiona.com/.

Julian of Norwich. *The Showings: Uncovering the Face of the Feminine in Revelations of Divine Love.* Translated by Mirabai Starr. Charlottesville, VA: Hampton Roads, 2022.

May, Gerald. "Angels at the Edge," *Shalem News*, Fall 1995.

Monastery of St. Clare. "Who We Are." https://poorclaresc.com/who-we-are-2/.

National Trust for Scotland. "Iona." https://www.nts.org.uk/visit/places/iona.

Nepo, Mark. *The Book of Awakening: Having the Life You Want by Being Present to the Life You Have.* Berkeley: Conari, 2000.

Newell, J. Philip. *Listening for the Heartbeat of God: A Celtic Spirituality.* New York: Paulist, 1997.

———. "Sacred Compassion: George MacLeod." In *Sacred Earth, Sacred Soil: Celtic Wisdom for Reawakening to What Our Souls Know and Healing the World*, 193–219. New York: HarperOne, 2021.

———. "Sacred Feminine: St. Brigid of Kildare." In *Sacred Earth, Sacred Soil: Celtic Wisdom for Reawakening to What Our Souls Know and Healing the World*, 45-70. New York: HarperOne, 2021.

Niemier, Roch. *In the Footsteps of Francis and Clare.* Cincinnati, OH: Franciscan, 2006.

Nezhukumatahil, Aimee. "More than Bird, Bees, and Trees: A Closer Look at Writing Haibun." Poets.org, February 20, 2014. https://poets.org/text/more-birds-bees-and-trees-closer-look-writing-haibun.

Paintner, Christine Valters. "Brigid of Kildare: The Healer." In *Illuminating the Way: Embracing the Wisdom of Monks and Mystics*, 83–98. Notre Dame, IN: Ave Marie, 2016.

———. "Hildegard of Bingen: The Visionary." In *Illuminating the Way: Embracing the Wisdom of Monks and Mystics*, 161–76. Notre Dame, IN: Ave Marie, 2016.

———. *Illuminating the Way: Embracing the Wisdom of Monks and Mystics.* Notre Dame, IN: Ave Marie, 2016.

Rilke, Rainer Maria. *Rilke's Book of Hours: Love Poems to God.* Translated by Anita Barrows and Joanna Macy. New York: Riverhead, 2005.

Robbins, Jim. *The Man Who Planted Trees: Lost Groves, Champion Trees, and an Urgent Plan to Save the Planet.* New York: Spiegel & Grau, 2012.

Rohr, Richard. *Eager to Love: The Alternative Way of Francis of Assisi.* Cincinnati, OH: Franciscan, 2014.

Rost Architecture Interiors. "The History of Gothic Cathedrals: The Architecture of Light," June 3, 2024. https://www.rostarchitects.com/articles/2024/5/29/the-gothic-era-the-evolution-of-a-new-architecture.

Rutherfurd, Edward. *Sarum: The Novel of England.* New York: Ballantine, 1997.

Salisbury Cathedral. "Salisbury Cathedral." https://www.salisburycathedral.org.uk/

Saint Francis Springs. "Our Story." https://www.stfrancis.today/our-story.

Schmitz, Britta. "Iona's Places of Sacred Pilgrimage and Ritual." Findhorn Foundation, November 26. https://www.findhorn.org/blog/ionas-places-of-sacred-pilgrimage-and-ritual.

Sims, Bennett J. *Servanthood: Leadership for the Third Millennium.* Eugene, OR: Wipf & Stock, 2005.

Starr, Mirabai. "Introduction." In *The Interior Castle* by Teresa of Ávila, translated by Mirabai Starr, 2–27. New York: Riverhead, 2003.

———. *Wild Mercy: Living the Fierce and Tender Wisdom of the Women Mystics.* Boulder: Sounds True, 2019.

Sweeney, John M. "Francis's Canticle of the Creatures." In *The St. Clare Prayer Book: Listening for God's Leading,* 153–54. Brewster, MA: Paraclete, 2007.

———. *The St. Clare Prayer Book: Listening for God's Leading.* Brewster, MA: Paraclete, 2007.

Taylor, Barbara Brown. *An Altar in the World: A Geography of Faith.* New York: HarperCollins, 2009.

———. *Holy Envy: Finding God in the Faith of Others.* New York: HarperOne, 2019.

———. *Leaving Church: A Memoir of Faith.* New York: HarperCollins, 2006.

Teasdale, Wayne. *The Mystic Heart: Discovering a Universal Spirituality in the World's Religions.* Novato, CA: New World Library, 1999.

Teresa of Ávila. *The Interior Castle.* Translated by Mirabai Starr. New York: Riverhead, 2003.

Thoman, Bret. "Leprosy and Minority." In *St. Francis of Assisi: Passion, Poverty, and the Man Who Transformed the Catholic Church,* 46–59. Charlotte, NC: TAN, 2018.

———. *St. Clare of Assisi: Light from the Cloister.* Charlotte, NC: TAN, 2017.

———. *St. Francis of Assisi: Passion, Poverty, and the Man Who Transformed the Catholic Church.* Charlotte, NC: TAN, 2018.

Trevanian. *Shibumi.* New York: Ballantine, 1983.

Veriditas. "Labyrinth Resources." https://veriditas.org/Labyrinth-Resources.

Vest, Douglas. *On Pilgrimage.* Cambridge, MA: Cowley, 1998.

Wolman, Richard N. *Thinking with Your Soul: Spiritual Intelligence and Why It Matters.* New York: Harmony, 2001.

www.ingramcontent.com/pod-product-compliance
Lightning Source LLC
LaVergne TN
LVHW020650100826
845148LV00012B/2420
* 9 7 9 8 3 8 5 2 6 5 4 7 3 *